Collected Haiku

Yannis Livadas

Collected Haiku

copyright © 2020 Yannis Livadas
ISBN 978-1-947271-66-1

Red Moon Press
PO Box 2461
Winchester VA
22604-1661 USA
www.redmoonpress.com

first printing

In memoriam Lucien Stryk

Introduction

These haiku were written in the period 1991–1997. All these years only a part of them were read by only one person; the late Lucien Stryk, with whom I was corresponding for several years. He wrote a few lines for these haiku, for which the appropriate time to be published is now, exactly the same as the haiku themselves, since for all these years both were deliberately left in a drawer:

> "Yannis Livadas has written a remarkable group of haiku. He is very close in spirit to Issa, one of haiku's Great Four, with the same humor, compassion, and tenderness, yet he is very much as writer his own man. His haiku would appeal, I'm confident, to all who care for the art, and he deserves a large readership. It takes a very special sensibility to create such a fine body of poetry, and at every turn in the group one finds evidence of just such a sensibility. It would be most difficult for me to single out favourite pieces, for I am impressed by all of the poems. Yannis Livadas

> is to be congratulated on his achievement, a very real one, and he should be read for the sheer pleasure of his work."

My essays on the nature of haiku and its aesthetic distinction have been previously published, absorbed up to some point, even as unendurable evidence, by those who have occasionally or somehow systematically, been engaged or interested in haiku. I have nothing to add to, nor to support anything further. Poetry is rather a lost cause recorded in the intellectual and psychological lists of necessities of some people, according to a series of directions they have chosen to live with and through.

Poetry and, more specifically, haiku, as phenomena not subject to the claims reproduced within the existential convention that people usually process; continue to inherit themselves, their idiom and emptiness, differently and independently of what is usually valued on the preponderant conventional scale. Haiku, for example, is not what anyone asks to be, or what anybody insists on being. There is no need for such will or for such perseverance. It would be much better for one to start tossing aside everything he knows about life and himself; then a glimpse of his absence may appear.

Haiku, I would say, is something that is due while at the same time it does not exist, and if a nugget of its nature ends up to man, it is only its unconceivable meaning, which as such has nothing more to offer than a jolt to his feasibility and mortality.

—Yannis Livadas
Paris 2020

Collected Haiku

He's sweeping
  fallen years
in the garden.

The sights
of the first
fallen half-leaf.

Relevance:
how moon
is a moon.

Rusted tin;
June, then
December.

Autumn is one
of the four,
no.

The moon
of someone's
autumn.

Desolation
broke the
mist hurtles.

Only leaves.
The tree is
somewhere.

The mountain,
by pointing
the cloud.

The voice
of the cat;
skilled in man.

All of them
to fall.
Still blossoms.

Whitened
signpost;
mist.

On the hillside
thin obliquity
of trees.

Waves
hate minced
words.

The door;
both sides
stand for.

The candle
responds kindly
to its flame.

Aspen's
autumn—
aspen.

Mist:
all ahead
forgotten.

End of the year;
    I want to
  pet the cat.

Moonlight;
yet moon
and light.

Full moon—
I have three eyes
indeed.

Roadtrip:
bird on hood
for an instant.

Listening to
songs; I recall
mouths.

A feather in
the stream,
of thought adrift.

Stars,
lights, even
my cigarette.

The old bum
as if he spoke
to the moon.

The art of
the mute trees
is told.

Whose blood

comes out,

poppies?

The cuckoo
sings his life
to the light rain.

He throws
a stone towards
his conceit.

At the end of
a grave parley;
crescent moon.

A dead
lighthouse,
under the moon.

The reeds
on the edge;
edging.

A dog's voice
barks to
nowhere.

Mountain;
pitch black
void of pines.

When said
the cuckoo
that I can?

A dog sniffed
the flower and
pissed it.

Grass
parts the road
in two.

The rock
on the sand;
a purpose.

Sun set.
Wind ceased;
childish silence.

Pain;
feeling the night
as man's night.

The wind
grabbed the road
from his feet.

The moon must
also be unseen;
even so.

The dog
chases his fear
of the huge train.

Bird! Don't
eat that fly!
It's Issa.

Sudden rain;
the eaves with
the garbage cans.

A sun sets
in cop's
sunglasses.

Outstripping
of moon and train;
daybreaking.

Simple life:
cat stares the fly
in peace.

The unbearable
　　jabber of
　the still bell.

　　The sound
　　of the rose
　beats silence.

The cemetery
birds and trees
get no glances.

Faint footprints
on the sand:
fearless spring.

Time
bothers routine's
stability.

Tiny buds get
the first lessons
in life.

By trimming
the trees you change
the sea.

The murmur
of the waves
is not of the sea.

One single row:
remote chairs,
skiffs, ropes.

Blooming wood
in the hearth;
cold fire.

The bird
regards the twig
as a work of art.

The lamp
receives gnats
as fireflies.

Granny holds
two copies of the
new calendar.

The blackbird!
yet the cricket
continues.

Our wind
brought a guest
wind.

The daze
of the summit
under a cloud.

Shooting star;
child, toy-spade
and bucket.

The shadow
of the cactus
attempts.

The grieving
poplar
gets worse.

Springtime;
the cleaner feet
of the sparrow.

Betwixt us
dry leaves
are hurrying.

The lamp's out;
    sparrow is
our only light.

No further
signification
from the chaff.

The shadow
over the well
is freezing.

If I pretend
I care; the poplar
does the same.

A notion
off something
in the dark.

Turns of
paged numbered
emptiness.

Whose god
is the
May beetle?

The wind
releases voices
of the trees.

Side by side,
green grapes
unripe teats.

These poplars
have something
in mind.

Timid clouds
circling the
full moon.

The mirror
receives dawns
and sunsets too.

That bird
is the
daybreak?

A slope:
mist and
moon roll.

A tiny mirror
gives me
the fisheye.

Rain;
threads the
wind weaves.

Some
hung flags
some hung wash.

Night action;
the poet and
the baker.

Waves summon
a man on account
of his time.

His eyes
take him for
a silent walk.

Since there's
a turn for every
straight line.

Smoke's
mouth through
his mouth.

The hand
of the haiku
budges.

This rain
is a few rains
together.

The butt
gets a life
in the gutter.

Words
express the sadness
of language.

Style;
one cat's
tail.

New Year's Eve;
   warm loafs,
fallen sesame.

Weeds down
below for the
time being.

The cat
stalks
no-thing.

The hint in
the dimples of
the baby.

Man

cat

fishbones.

The statue
is guarding
a watchman.

Water
with a glass
of.

For an instant
the moment
got me.

Full moon;
all the rest try,
but break.

The flowers
of her robe were
hiding flowers.

The leaf
and the bug;
or vice versa?

Fleeting
in my own
time.

The life
of words:
a man writes.

Whatever it
may be that's
exactly is.

Performance
of tray on
waiter's palm.

Bridge's
dispute over
the river.

Wind and grave;
razor and
whetstone.

His oblivion
cloisters in
repetition.

The fly
becomes a fly
by sucking.

The mute
mimics
Charlie Parker.

The wind blows
only for her skirt,
her legs.

The fragment
from the glass
tranquil.

Staircases:
always with two
end-points.

Seasons
serving time
for my life.

The way the curses
of the nightingale
are heard.

New autumn
scratches
old thoughts.

The neighbor sucks
sunshine with
a vacuum cleaner.

The broken one;
    indifferent to
its stray pieces.

Delos island—
past and future
    impacted.

Acts abuzz
into Time's
strongbox.

Big toe's hairs
stand also against
emptiness.

Dawn breaks
not melodic;
said the blackbird.

Paper, ink:
a poem's
funeral.

BIBLIOGRAPHY

Kemiklerimden Yapılma Mezar Çorbası [*Seçilmiş kısa şiirler 1996–2012*] (Sub Press, Türkiye 2020)

La Chope Daguerre / Autoreportage (Edizioni Kolibris, Italia 2020)

My Bones In The Soup Of My Grave: Selected Shorter Poems 1996–2012 (Ragged Lion Press, United Kingdom 2019)

A Sum of Haiku: 1991–1997 (Ragged Lion Press, United Kingdom 2019)

Autoreportages (Moloko Print, Germany 2018)

Haiku 1991–2008 (Ekati, Greece 2018)

Inferred Emptiness (Koukoutsi, Greece 2017)

Magnat De La Mort [*Poèmes courts 1997–2011*] (Éditions L' Harmattan, France 2017)

Yannis Livadas interviewed by Ben Schot and Five Poems (A co-edition of Moloko Print and Sea Urchin Editions (Germany/Netherlands 2017)

Austerity Measures/The New Greek Poetry [is included with six poems] (New York Review Books, USA 2017)

Austerity Measures/The New Greek Poetry [is included with six poems] (Penguin Books, UK 2016)

Modart (Alloglotta Editions, Greece 2015)

Strictly Two (Sea Urchin Editions, Netherlands 2015)

The fat of the fly (Kedros, Greece 2015)

Sound Bones [*17 poems for Jazz*] (Iolkos, Greece 2014)

La Chope Daguerre + Tusk Poems (Kedros, Greece 2013)

Bezumljie (Peti Talas, Serbia 2012)

Ravaged By The Hand Of Beauty (Cold Turkey Press, France 2012)

Kelifus (Cold Turkey Press, France 2011)

Ati — Scattered Poems 2001–2009 (Kedros, Greece 2011)

The Margins Of A Central Man (Graffiti Kolkata, India 2010)

The Star Electric Space/An International Anthology Of Indie Writers [is included with 4 poems] (Graffiti Kolkata, India 2010)

John Coltrane & 15 Poems for Jazz (C.C. Marimbo, USA 2008)

Apteral Nike / Business / Sphinx (Heridanos, Greece 2008)

John Coltrane and 12 Poems for Jazz (Apopeira, Greece 2007)

The Hanging Verses Of Babylon (Melani, Greece 2007)

Annex of Temperate Emotion (Indiktos, Greece 2003)

Receipt of Retail Poetry (Akron, Greece 2002)

Expressionistic Feedback (Akron, Greece 2000)

YANNIS LIVADAS is a contemporary Greek poet, born in 1969. In 1993 he invented the "fusion-sonnet". In 2008 he came up with the idea of "organic antimetathesis", the transpositional synthesis of poetry based on the scaling indeterminacy of meaning, of syntactic comparisons and structural contradistinction. He works as an editor, translator and independent scholar with a specialization in modernism, postmodernism, and haiku. He is also a columnist and freelance contributor to various literary magazines. His poems and essays have been translated into twelve languages. He lives in Paris, France.

Made in the USA
Middletown, DE
15 February 2021